What is coding

Author: Borth, Teddy.
Reading Level: 2.7 LG
Point Value: 0.5
ACCELERATED READER QUIZ 512487

D1712526

WHAT IS CODING?

by Teddy Borth

Cody Koala

An Imprint of Pop!
popbooksonline.com

abdobooks.com
Published by Pop!, a division of ABDO, PO Box 398166, Minneapolis,
Minnesota 55439. Copyright © 2022 by Abdo Consulting Group, Inc.
International copyrights reserved in all countries. No part of this book may
be reproduced in any form without written permission from the publisher.
Cody Koala™ is a trademark and logo of Pop!.

Printed in the United States of America, North Mankato, Minnesota

052021
092021

THIS BOOK CONTAINS
RECYCLED MATERIALS

Cover Photo: Shutterstock Images
Interior Photos: Shutterstock Images, 6, 9 (top), 9 (bottom left), 9 (bottom
center), 10, 14, 17, 19; iStockphotos, 13, 20

Editor: Elizabeth Andrews
Series Designer: Laura Graphenteen

Library of Congress Control Number: 2020948220
Publisher's Cataloging-in-Publication Data
Names: Borth, Teddy, author.
Title: What is coding? / by Teddy Borth
Description: Minneapolis, Minnesota : Pop!, 2022 | Series: Coding basics |
Includes online resources and index.
Identifiers: ISBN 9781532169663 (lib. bdg.) | ISBN 9781098240592 (ebook)
Subjects: LCSH: Coding theory--Juvenile literature. | Programming
languages (Electronic computers)--Juvenile literature. |
Computer programming--Juvenile literature.
Classification: DDC 005.1--dc23

Hello! My name is

Cody Koala

Pop open this book and you'll find QR codes like this one, loaded with information, so you can learn even more!

Scan this code* and others like it while you read, or visit the website below to make this book pop.

popbooksonline.com/what-is-coding

*Scanning QR codes requires a web-enabled smart device with a QR code reader app and a camera.

Table of Contents

Chapter 1
Reading Instructions. 4

Chapter 2
Writing Instructions 8

Chapter 3
Code in the World 12

Chapter 4
Human Codes. 18

Making Connections 22
Glossary. 23
Index 24
Online Resources 24

Reading Instructions

Code is a list of **instructions**. It tells the computer what to do. People write code for computers. Every app, website, and game is made with code.

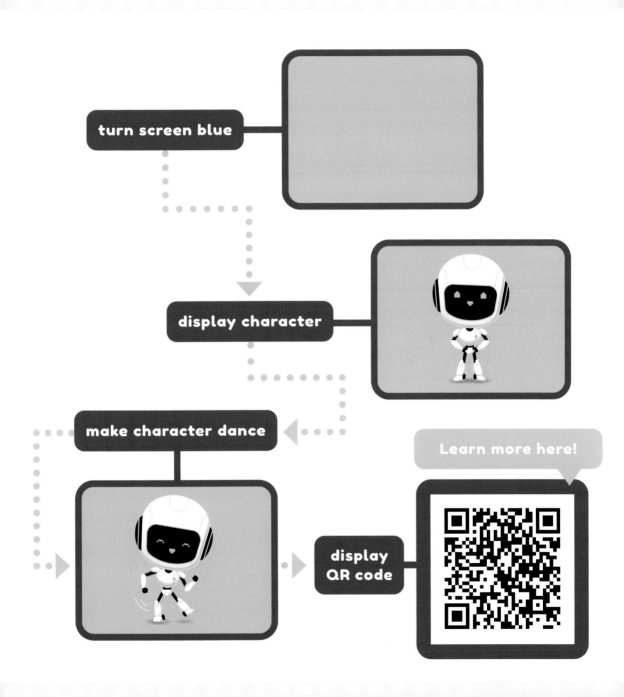

turn screen blue

display character

make character dance

display
QR code

Learn more here!

Computers can only do one thing at a time. They read code one line at a time. Even though computers can only do things one at a time, they do them very fast.

An average smartphone can do millions of operations each second!

Chapter 2

Writing Instructions

Dave is a **coder**. He is writing code for a **program**. This program will control his Christmas lights!

code

Watch a Video Here!

remote

Computers need code to function. They need to be told what to do and when to do it. Even simple things, like using a TV remote, use code.

Pressing a button on the remote completes a circuit inside. This sends a code to the TV. The TV decodes the signal and performs an action.

Chapter 3

Code in the World

Abby and her mom are at a **stoplight**. This light is coded to change on a timer. They have to wait until the code changes the light from red to green.

Holly is playing a video game. The game checks when a button is being pressed. Then it runs more code and performs an action on the TV. Holly doesn't care. She's just trying to get first place!

It takes a lot of **instructions** to run more advanced **programs**. Things like smartphones or even cars need millions of lines of code to perform properly.

00011100100010011100100100110010100

smartphone

00011100100010011100100100110010

Chapter 4

Human Codes

People write codes for themselves. A grocery list is a type of code. Amy helps her dad at the store. She "runs" the code by getting each item on the list.

Complete an activity here!

Before Sam can run, he has to wait for the batter to hit the ball. That starts the code!

Each sport uses code. These are the rules of the game! Sam follows the code during the baseball game. He knows when to run at the right times.

Making Connections

Text-to-Self

Rules, actions, and buttons are all codes used in games. Think of your favorite video or board games. What codes do you use to play them?

Text-to-Text

Have you read other books about coding? What did you learn?

Text-to-World

Computers and technology work because of people who are coders. How do coders know what to do?

Glossary

coder – a person who builds programs or works with computer languages.

instruction – directions or orders of what to do.

program – a collection of instructions that a computer uses to perform a task.

stoplight – a light at an intersection that tells drivers when to go, slow down, or stop.

Index

coder, 8

computer, 4, 7, 11

game, 4, 15, 21

program, 8, 16

smartphone, 7, 16–17

TV, 11, 15

Online Resources

popbooksonline.com

Thanks for reading this Cody Koala book!

Scan this code* and others like it in this book, or visit the website below to make this book pop!

popbooksonline.com/what-is-coding

*Scanning QR codes requires a web-enabled smart device with a QR code reader app and a camera.